RECORDED VERSIONS
GUITAR ®

AUTHENTIC TRANSCRIPTIONS
WITH NOTES AND TABLATURE

CREED
weathered

contents

Music transcriptions by Pete Billmann

ISBN 0-634-04429-X

HAL•LEONARD®
CORPORATION
7777 W. BLUEMOUND RD. P.O. BOX 13819 MILWAUKEE, WI 53213

Visit Hal Leonard Online at
www.halleonard.com

Photo by Sean Perry

Photo by Len Irish

Bullets

Words and Music by Mark Tremonti and Scott Stapp

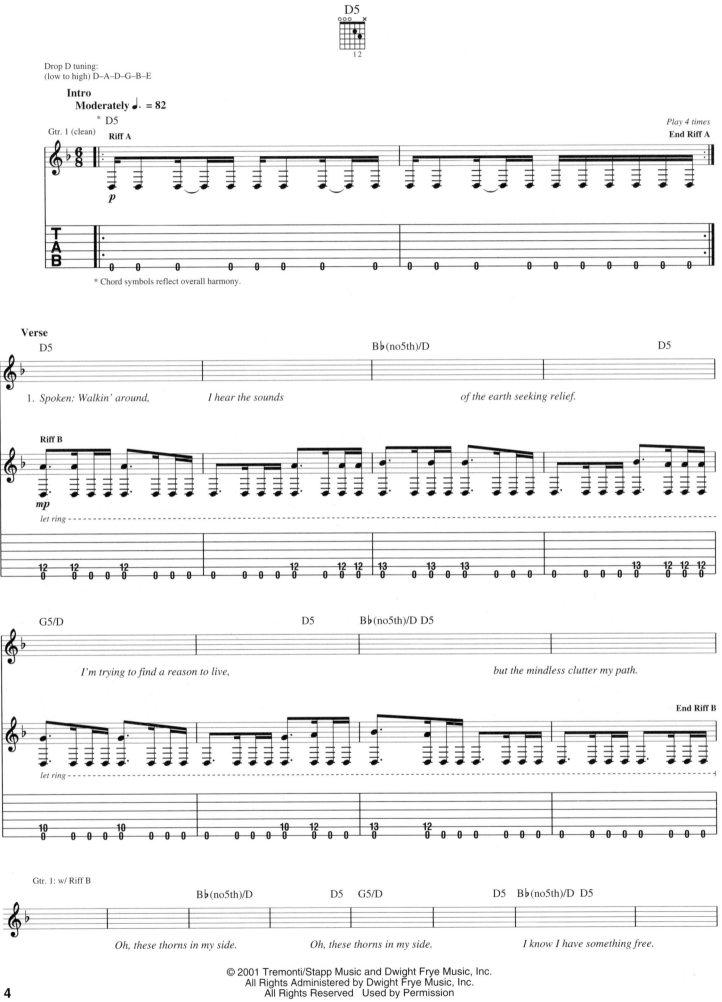

Drop D tuning:
(low to high) D–A–D–G–B–E

Intro
Moderately ♩. = 82

Gtr. 1 (clean)

*Chord symbols reflect overall harmony.

Verse

1. *Spoken: Walkin' around,*   *I hear the sounds*   *of the earth seeking relief.*

I'm trying to find a reason to live,   *but the mindless clutter my path.*

Gtr. 1: w/ Riff B

Oh, these thorns in my side.   *Oh, these thorns in my side.*   *I know I have something free.*

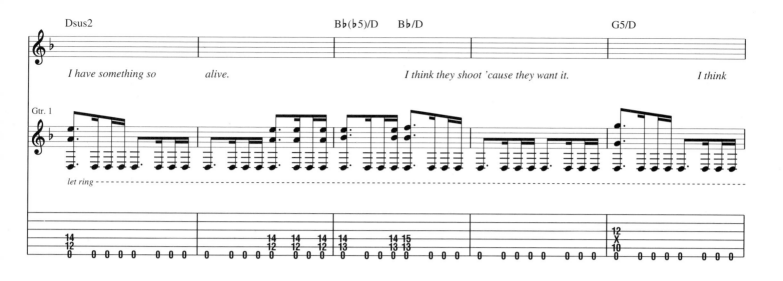

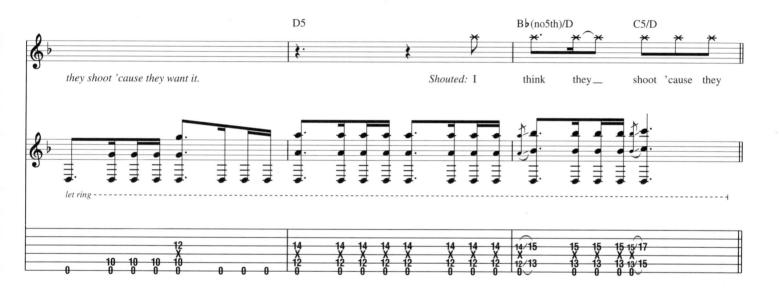

Interlude

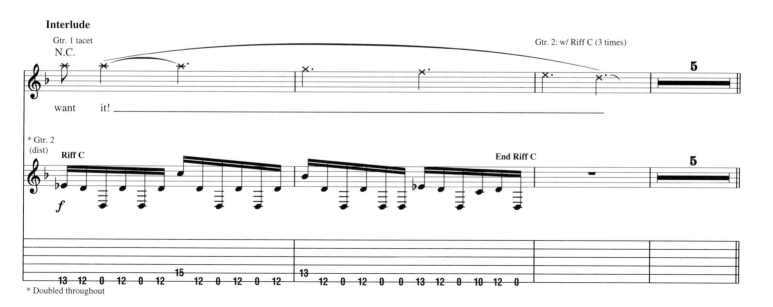

* Doubled throughout

Freedom Fighter

Words and Music by Mark Tremonti and Scott Stapp

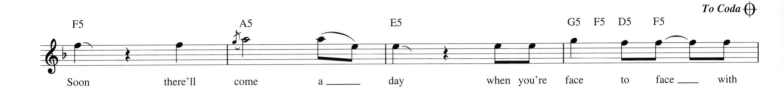

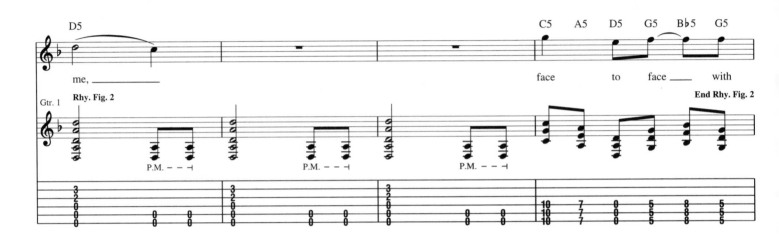

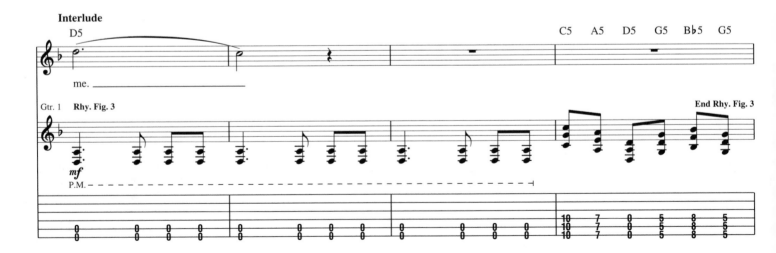

Bridge

Gtr. 1: w/ Rhy. Fig. 3 (3 times)

Can't you hear ___ us com - in'? Peo - ple march - in' all ___ a - round.

Can't you see ___ we're com - in'? Close your eyes, ___ it's o - ver now. ___

Can't you hear ___ us com - in? ___ The fight has on - ly just be - gun. ___

Can't you see ___ we're com - in? ___

Gtr. 1

Rhy. Fig. 4

Hey!

15

Who's Got My Back?

Words and Music by Mark Tremonti and Scott Stapp

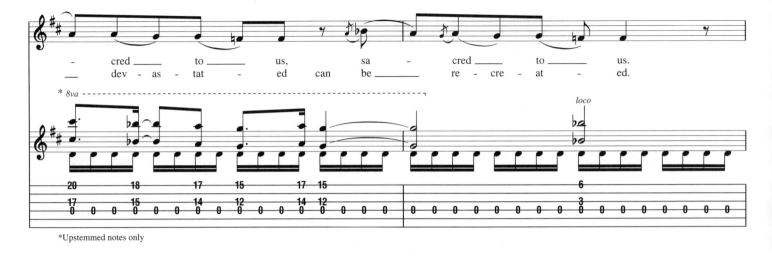

-cred ___ to ___ us, sa - cred ___ to ___ us.
___ dev - as - tat - ed can be ___ re - cre - at - ed.

*8va

loco

*Upstemmed notes only

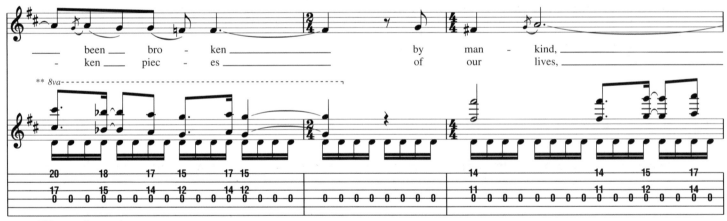

See the signs.   The cov - e - nant has
Re - al - ize   we pick up the bro -

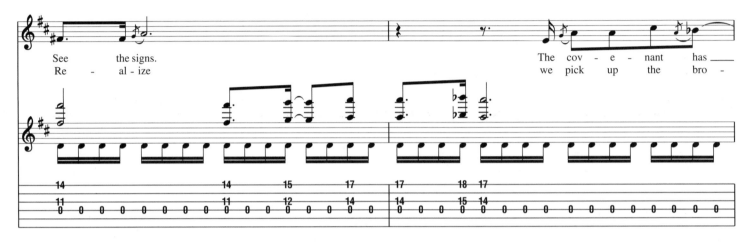

___ been ___ bro - ken ___   by man - kind, ___
- ken piec - es ___   of our lives, ___

**8va

**Upstemmed notes only

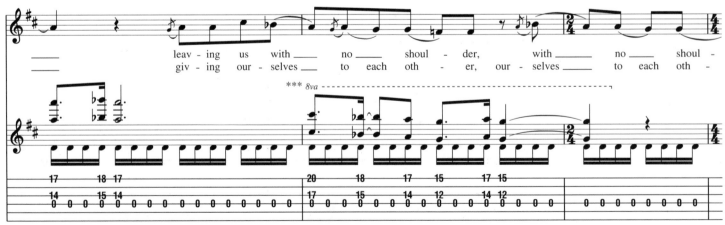

___ leav - ing us with ___ no ___ shoul - der, with ___ no ___ shoul -
- giv - ing our - selves ___ to each oth - er, our - selves ___ to each oth -

***8va

***Upstemmed notes only

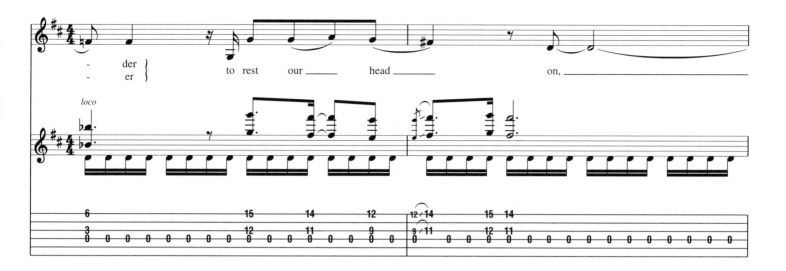

- der }
- er }
to rest our _____ head _____ on, _____

loco

To Coda 1 ⊕

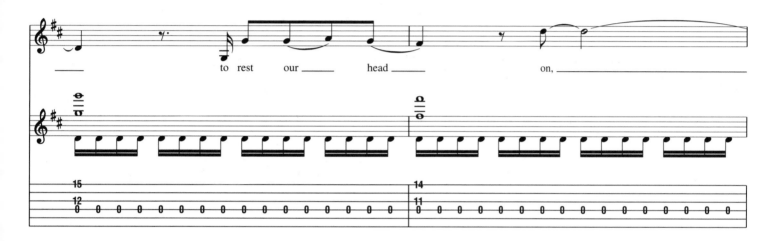

to rest our _____ head _____ on, _____

Interlude

D

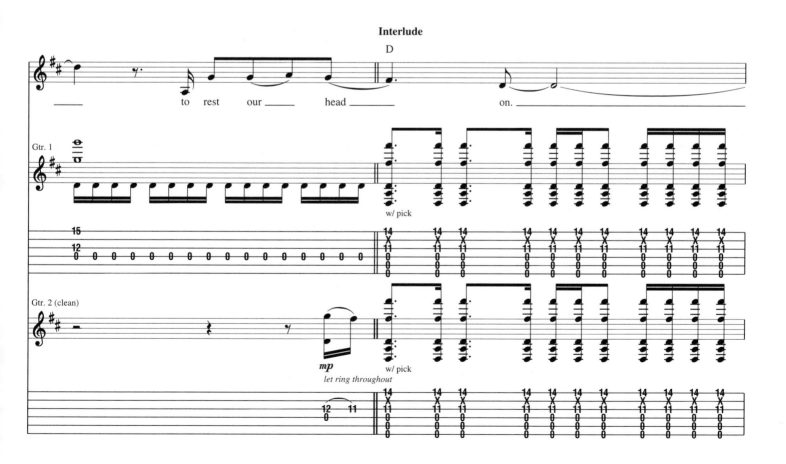

_____ to rest our _____ head _____ on.

Gtr. 1

w/ pick

Gtr. 2 (clean)

mp
let ring throughout

w/ pick

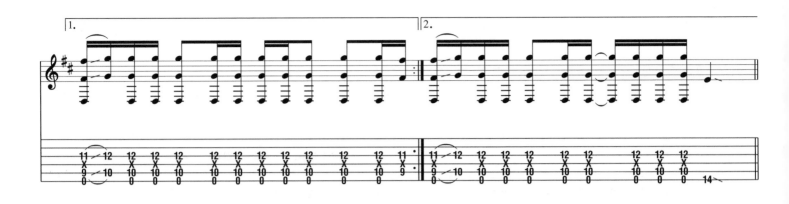

Bridge

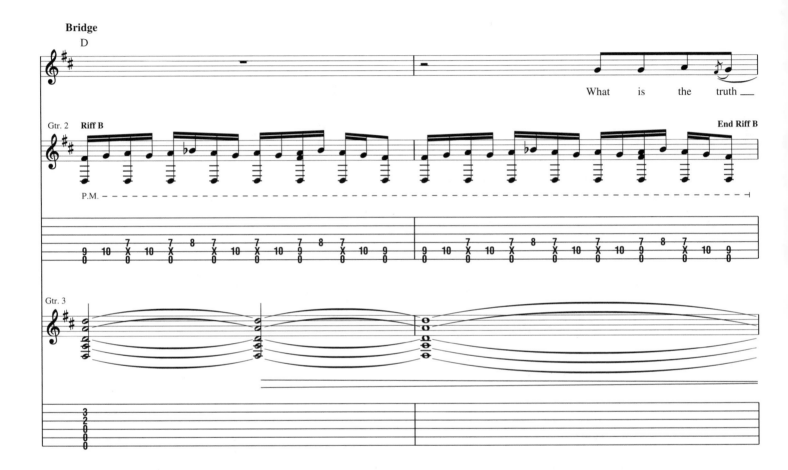

What is the truth ___

___ now? ___ Tell me the truth ___ now. ___

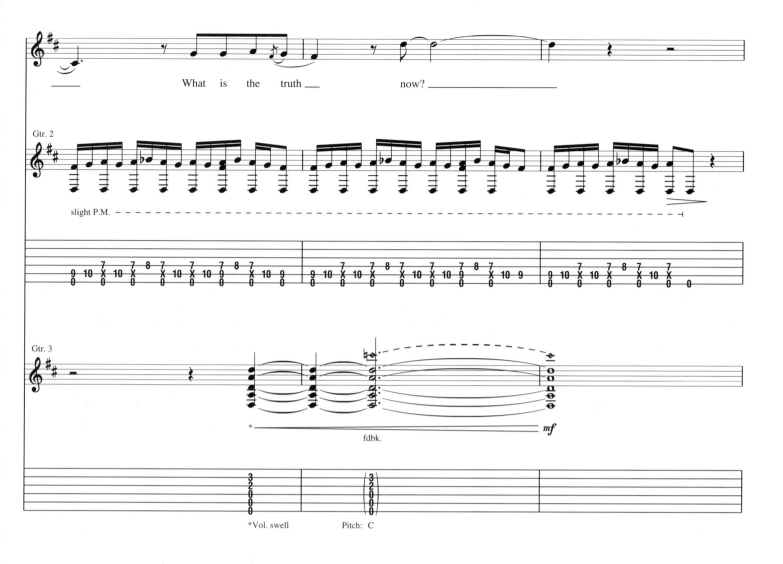

What is the truth ___ now? _____

*Vol. swell   Pitch: C

What is the truth ___

Gtr. 3: w/ Riff C

_____ now? _____ Tell us the truth. _____

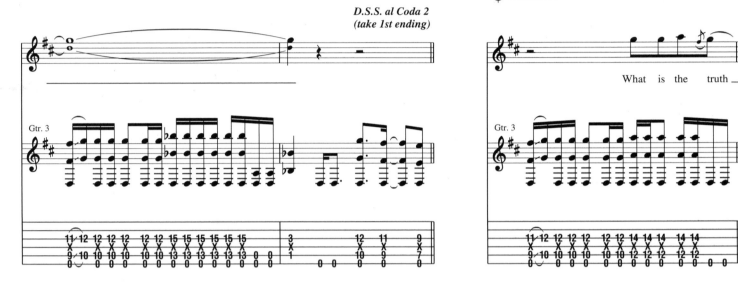

D.S.S. al Coda 2
(take 1st ending)

⊕ **Coda 2**

What is the truth _____

Gtr. 3

Gtr. 3

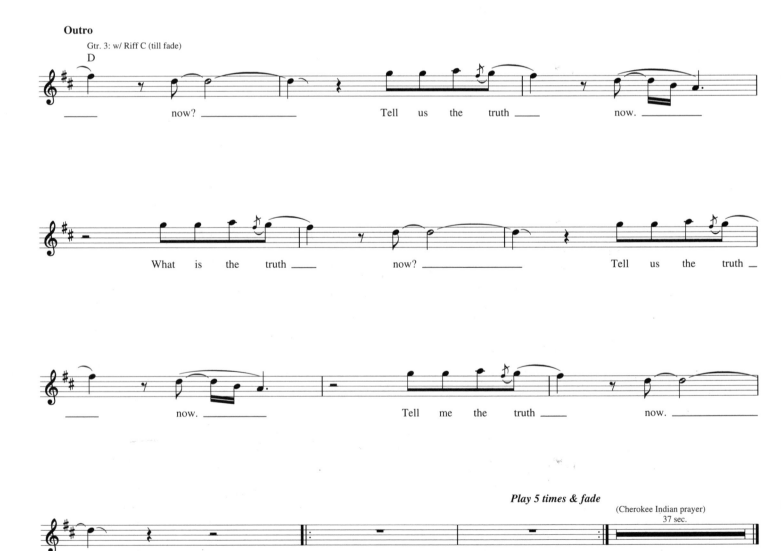

Outro

Gtr. 3: w/ Riff C (till fade)

D

_____ now? _____ Tell us the truth _____ now. _____

What is the truth _____ now? _____ Tell us the truth _____

_____ now. _____ Tell me the truth _____ now. _____

Play 5 times & fade

(Cherokee Indian prayer)
37 sec.

Signs

Words and Music by Mark Tremonti and Scott Stapp

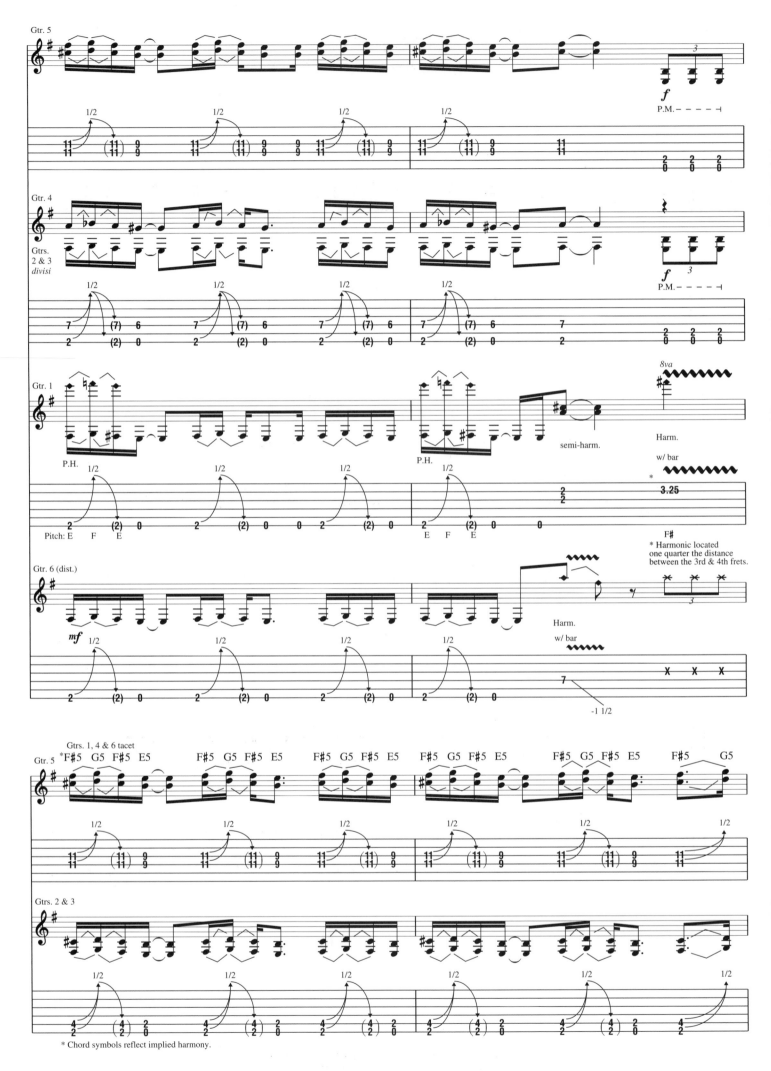

* Chord symbols reflect implied harmony.

Verse

1. This is not a - bout age.
2. This is not a - bout race,

Gtr. 5 **Rhy. Fig. 1A**

2nd time, Gtrs. 2 & 3: w/ Rhy. Fill 1

Gtr. 2

8va

rake

Harm.

*

Pitch: E   D

* Harmonic located three quarters the distance between the 2nd & 3rd frets.

Gtr. 3 **Rhy. Fig. 1**

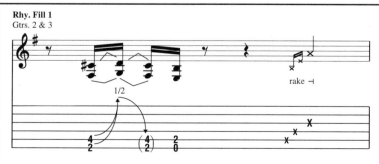

Rhy. Fill 1
Gtrs. 2 & 3

rake

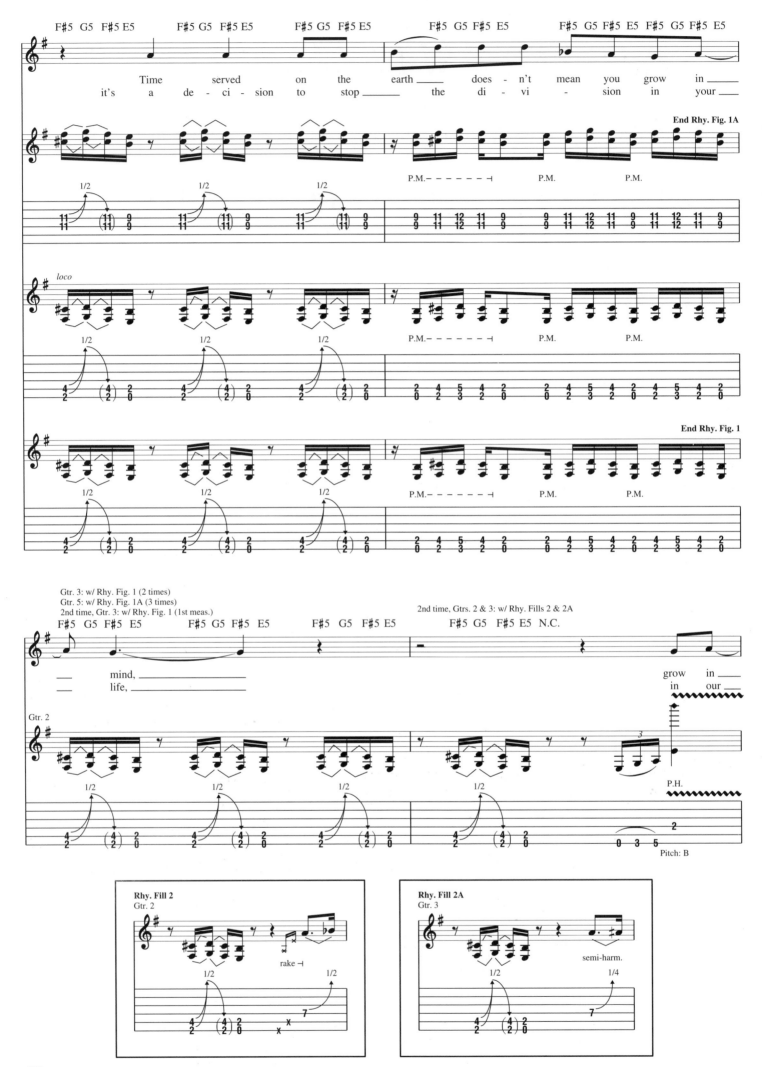

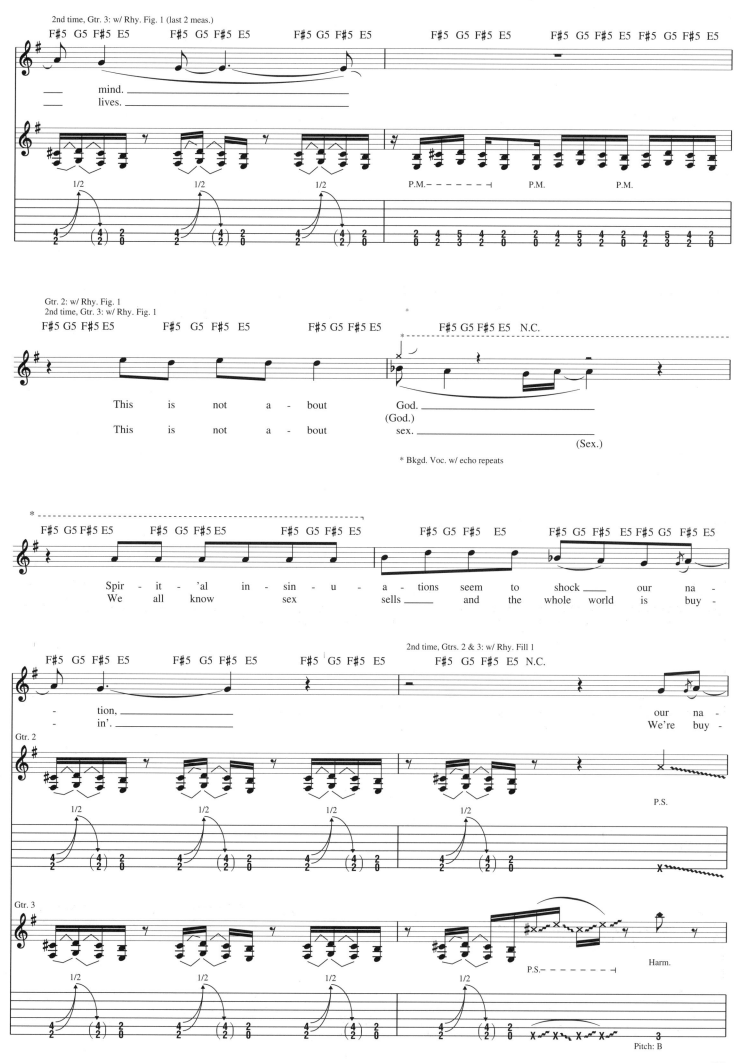

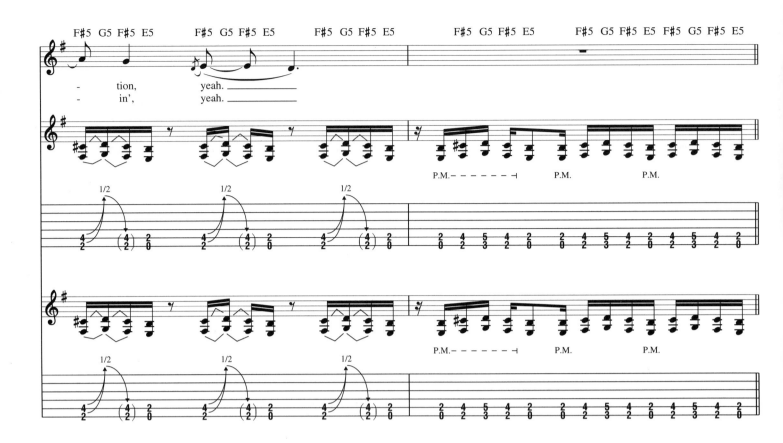

Chorus

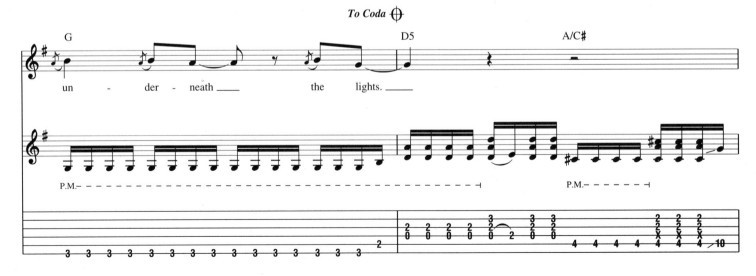

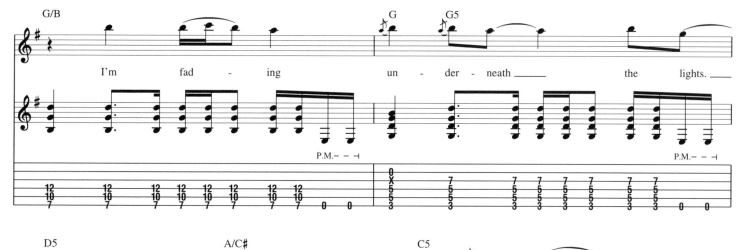

I'm fad - ing un - der - neath _____ the lights. _____

Come with _____ me,

come with _____ me, _____ come with _____ me now. _____

Outro

Gtrs. 2 & 3: w/ Rhy. Fig. 2 (3 1/2 times)

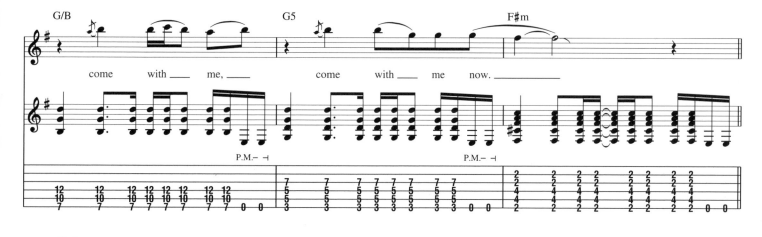

Can't you _____ see _____ them, see the signs? You _____ see _____ them, all the

signs, we _____ see _____ them. _____   signs, we _____ see _____ them. _____

Gtrs. 2 & 3

One Last Breath

Words and Music by Mark Tremonti and Scott Stapp

Intro
Slowly ♩ = 63

*Chord symbols reflect implied harmony.

Verse
Gtr. 1: w/ Riff A (2 times)

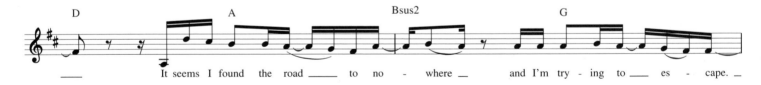

1. Please come now, __ I think I'm fall - ing. __ I'm hold-ing on to all I think __ is __ safe.

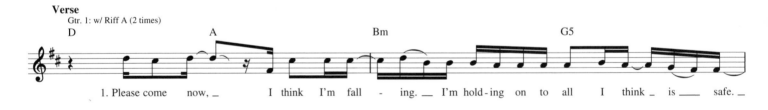

__ It seems I found the road __ to no - where __ and I'm try - ing to __ es - cape.

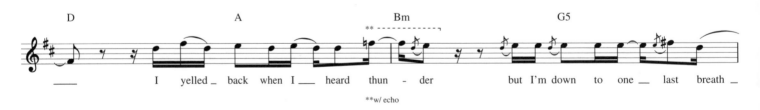

__ I yelled __ back when I __ heard thun - der but I'm down to one __ last breath __

**w/ echo

__ and with it, let __ me say, __ let me say... __

Chorus

Hold me now, I'm six feet from the edge and I'm think - ing

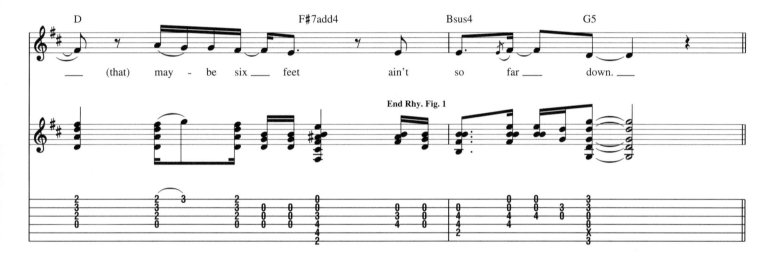

(that) may - be six feet ain't so far down.

Interlude

Gtr. 1: w/ Riff A

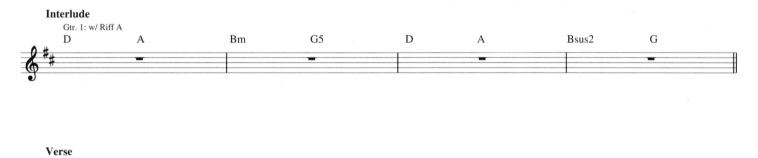

Verse

Gtr. 1: w/ Riff A (2 times)

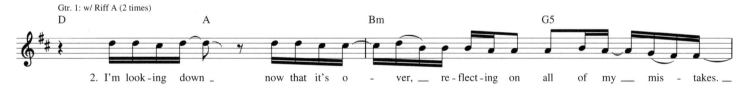

2. I'm look - ing down now that it's o - ver, re - flect - ing on all of my mis - takes.

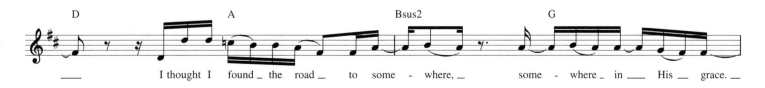

I thought I found the road to some - where, some - where in His grace.

I cried _ out, "Heav-en _ save _ me" but I'm down to one _ last breath _

*w/ echo

and with it, let _ me say, _____ let me say...

Gtr. 2 (dist.)

Pitch: A
*Harmonic located three-tenths the distance between 3rd and 4th frets.

Gtr. 3 (dist.)

𝄋 **Chorus**

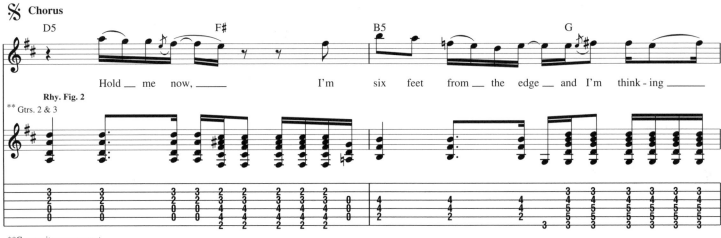

Hold _ me now, _____ I'm six feet from _ the edge _ and I'm think-ing _____

Rhy. Fig. 2
** Gtrs. 2 & 3

**Composite arrangement

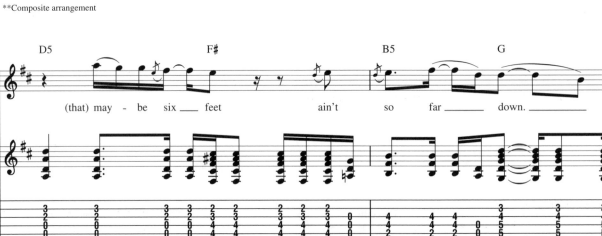

(that) may-be six _ feet ain't so far _____ down. _____

End Rhy. Fig. 2

Gtrs. 2 & 3: w/ Rhy. Fig. 2
2nd time, Gtrs. 2 & 3: w/ Rhy. Fig. 2 (1st 3 meas.)

D5   F♯   B5   G

Hold __ me now, _____ I'm six feet from __ the edge __ and I'm think - ing _____

To Coda ⊕

D5   F♯   B5   G

(that) may - be six __ feet ain't so far _____ down. _____

B5   G   B5   G

I'm so far _____ down. _____

Gtrs. 2 & 3

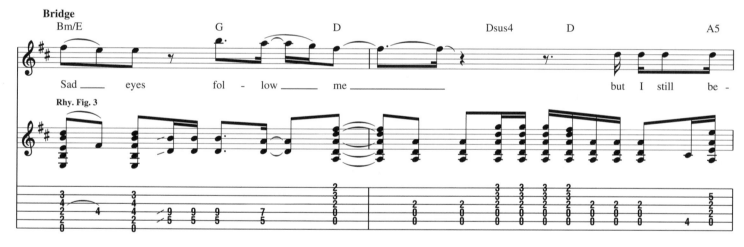

Bridge

Bm/E   G   D   Dsus4   D   A5

Sad _____ eyes fol - low _____ me _____ but I still be -

Rhy. Fig. 3

B5   G

lieve _____ there's some - thing left __ for me. _____ So

End Rhy. Fig. 3

please come stay ____ with ____ me ____ 'cause I still be -

lieve ____ there's some-thing left ____ for you and me, for you and me, for you and me. ____

Interlude

Gtr. 1: w/ Rhy. Fig. 1

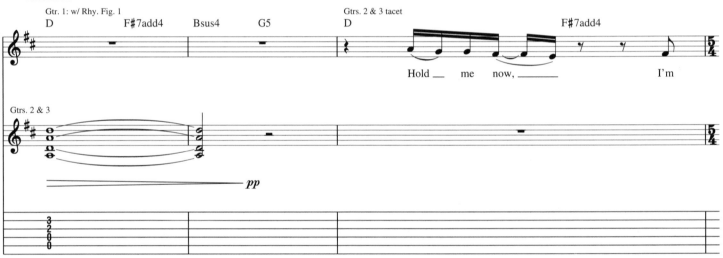

Hold ____ me now, _____ I'm

D.S. al Coda

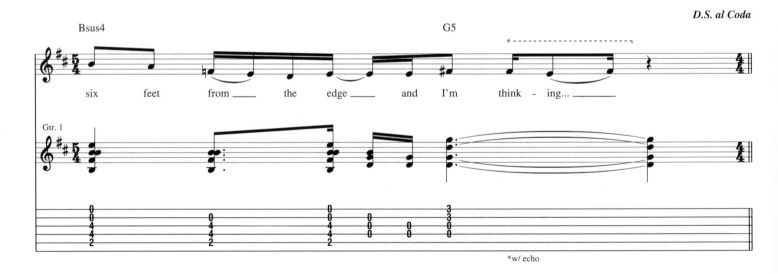

six feet from ____ the edge ____ and I'm think - ing... _____

*w/ echo

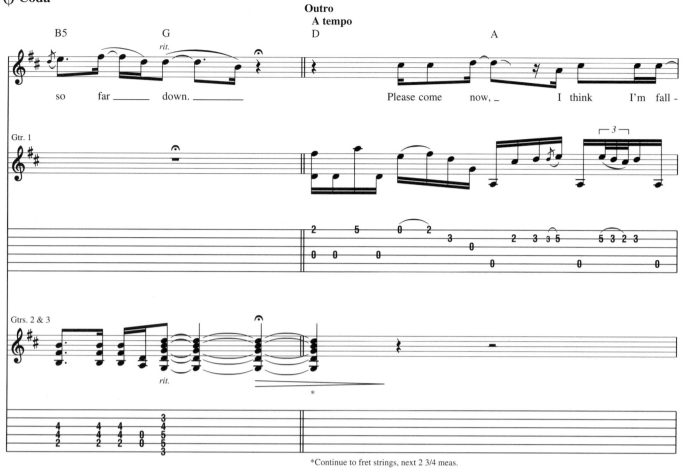

My Sacrifice

Words and Music by Mark Tremonti and Scott Stapp

Verse

lo _ my friend, _ we meet a - gain. _ It's been a while; _ where _ should we _ be - gin? _
seen _ our share _ of ups _ and downs. _ Oh, how quick-ly life _ can turn _ a - round _

_ It feels like _ for - ev - er. _ With -
_ in an in - stant. _ It

in _ my heart _ are mem - o - ries _ of per - fect love that _ you gave _ to me. _
feels _ so good to re - u - nite, _ with - in _ your - self _ and with - in _ your mind. _

Oh, I re - mem - ber. _ When you are _ }
Let's find peace _ there. _ 'Cause when you are _ }

P.S.

𝄋 Chorus

3rd time, Gtrs. 1 & 2 tacet
3rd time, Gtr. 3: w/ Rhy. Fill 1

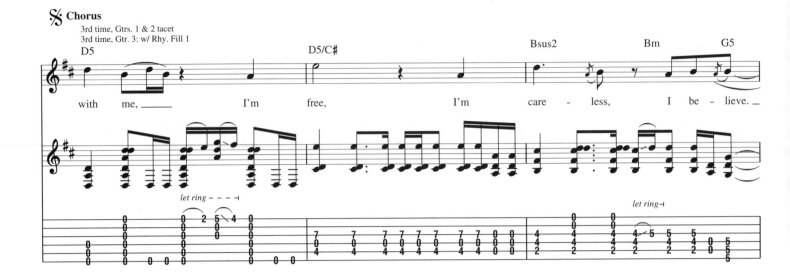

with me, _____ I'm free, I'm care - less, I be - lieve. _____

3rd time, Gtr. 3: w/ Rhy. Fill 2

A - bove all the oth - ers _____ we'll

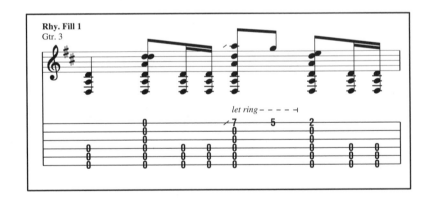

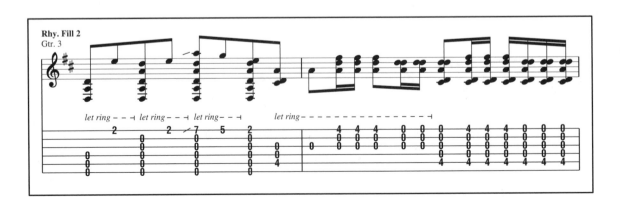

Bridge

Gtr. 3: w/ Riff A (3 times)

I just want to say hel - lo a - gain.

I just want to say hel - lo a - gain.

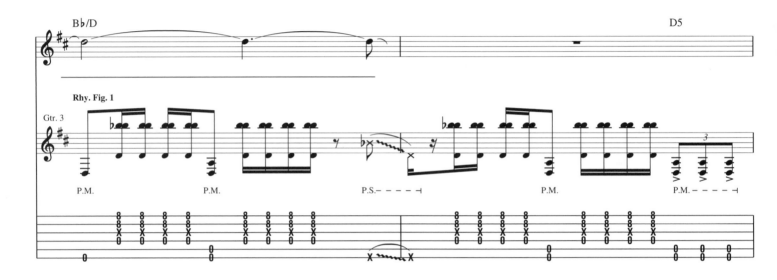

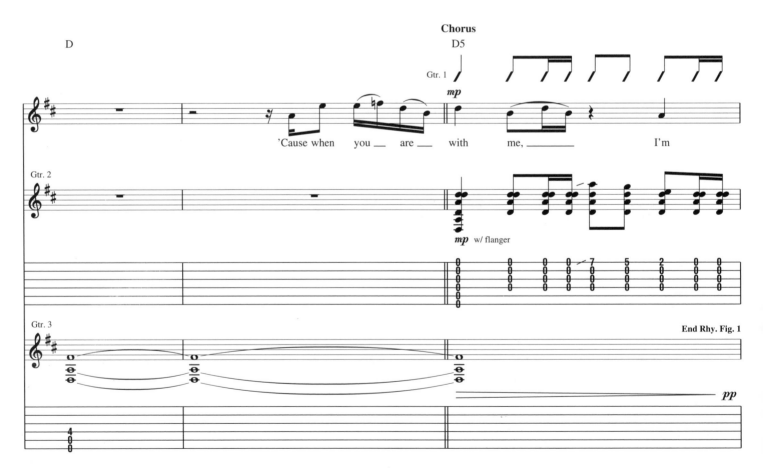

Chorus

'Cause when you are with me, I'm

44

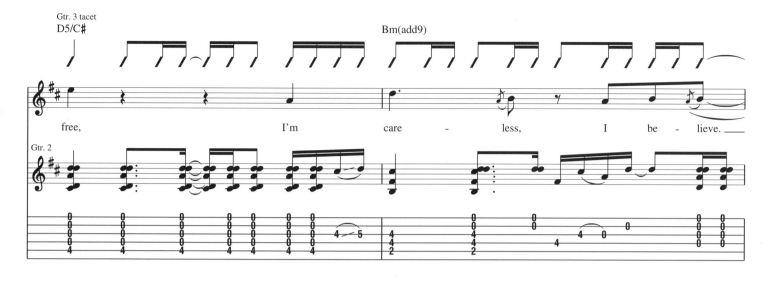

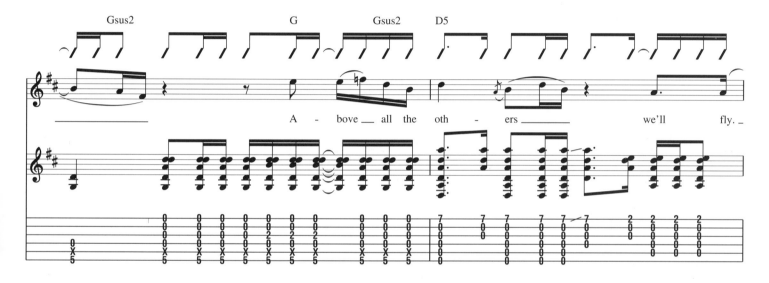

⊕ Coda

Bridge

Gtr. 3: w/ Riff A (3 times)

My sac - ri - fice. _____ (I just want ___ to say ___

I ___ just want ___ to say ___ hel - lo a - gain.

_____ hel - lo _____ a-gain.)

Gtr. 3: w/ Rhy. Fig. 1

My sac - ri - fice. _____

Outro

Begin fade

Gtr. 4 (elec.)

mp

w/ slight dist.

let ring throughout

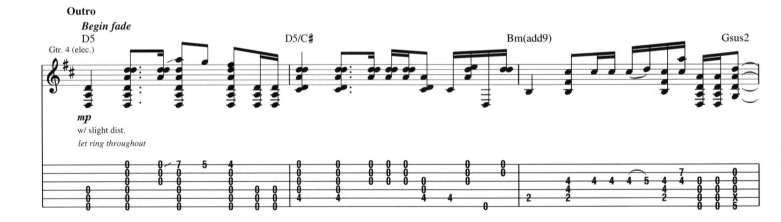

Fade out

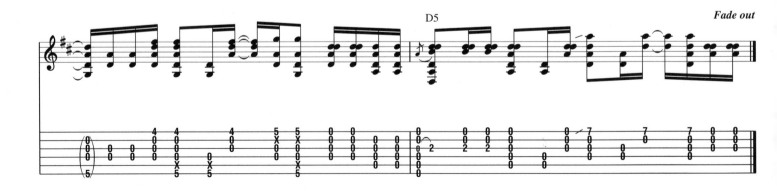

Stand Here With Me

Words and Music by Mark Tremonti and Scott Stapp

* Chord symbols reflect implied harmony.

** Composite arrangement

1. You al - ways reached __ out to me, and helped __ me be - lieve. ____

'Cause you stand here with me

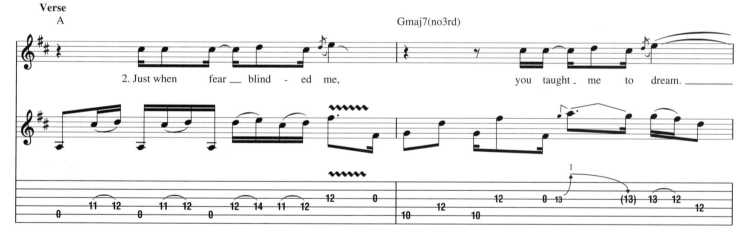

now, _____ yeah. __

Verse

2. Just when fear __ blind - ed me, you taught __ me to dream. __

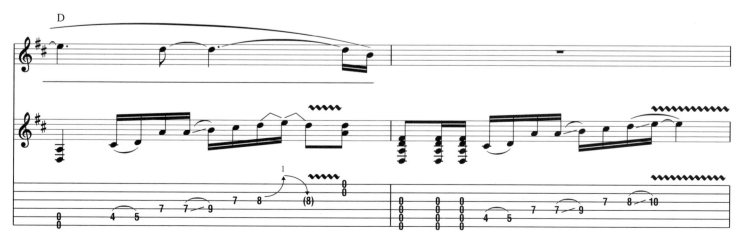

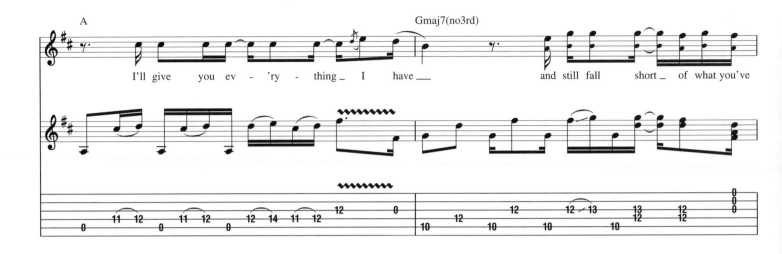

I'll give you ev - 'ry - thing _ I have _ and still fall short _ of what you've

done for me. _____ In this

Gtrs. 2 & 3: w/ Riff B

life that I live, _____ I hope I can give _____ love un -

Gtrs. 2 & 3: w/ Riff A (1st 2 meas.)

self - ish - ly. _____ I've learned the world _ is big - ger than

Gtrs. 2 & 3: w/ Riff C

me. _ You're my dai - ly dose _ of re - al - i - ty. _ 'Cause

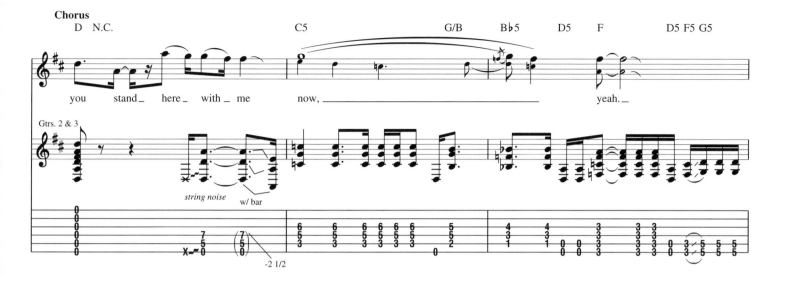

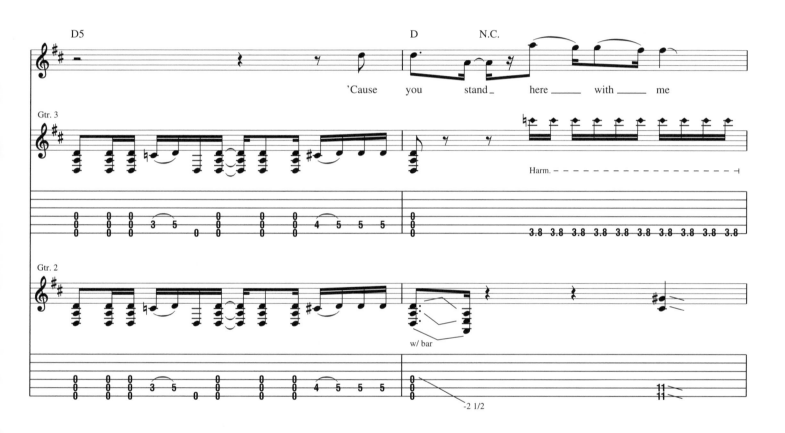

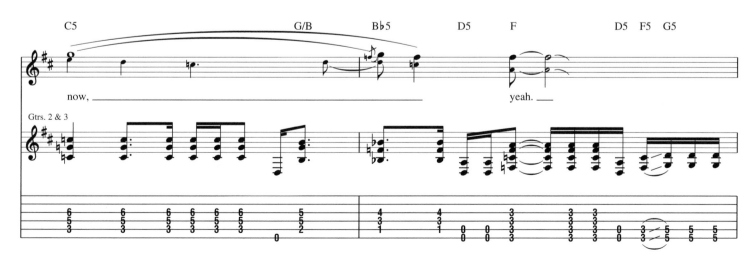

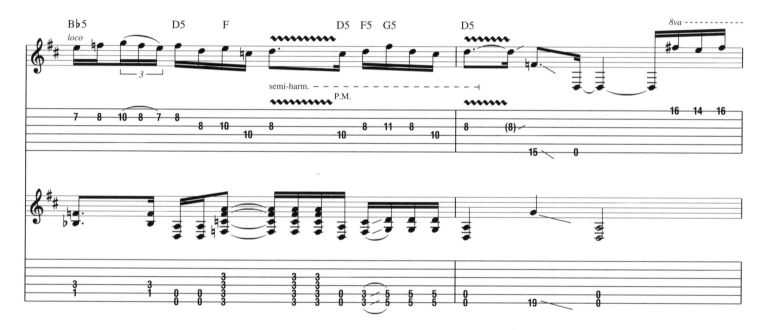

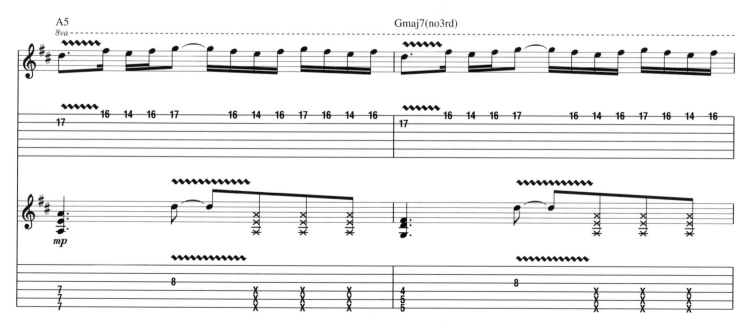

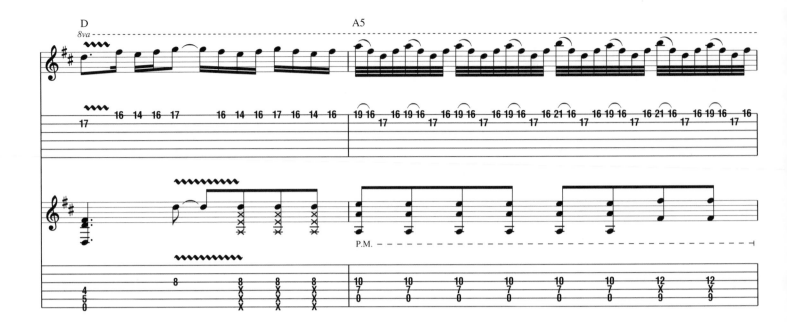

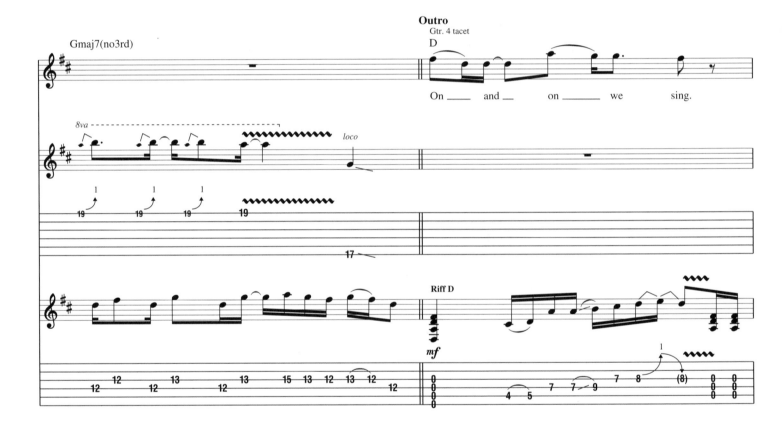

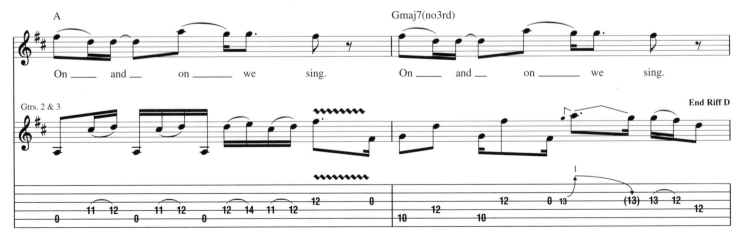

Weathered

Words and Music by Mark Tremonti and Scott Stapp

Tuning:
(low to high) D–A–D–A–D–D

Intro
Moderately slow ♩ = 72

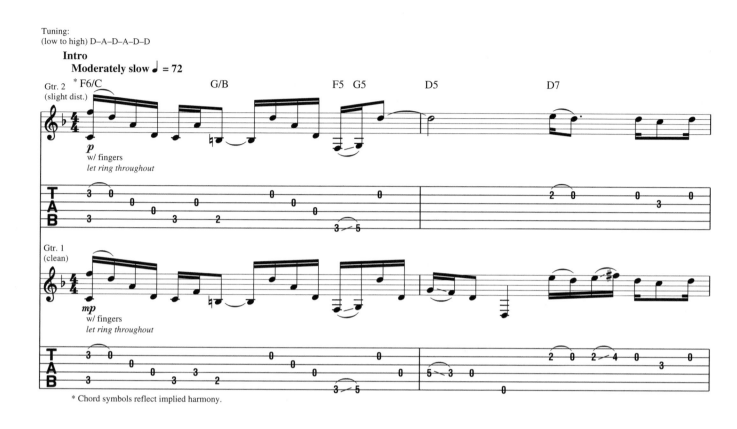

* Chord symbols reflect implied harmony.

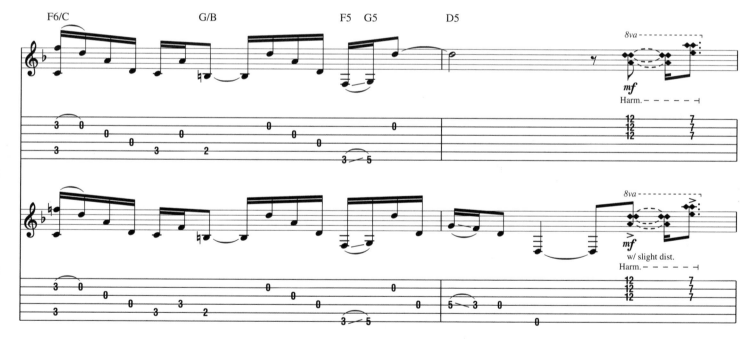

** Composite arrangement
*** Chord symbols reflect overall harmony.

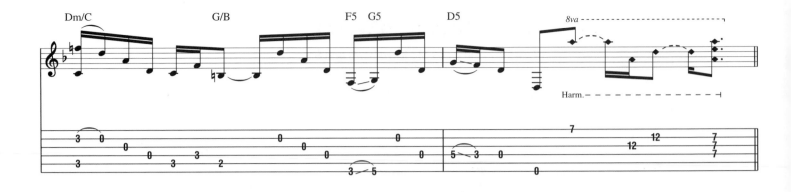

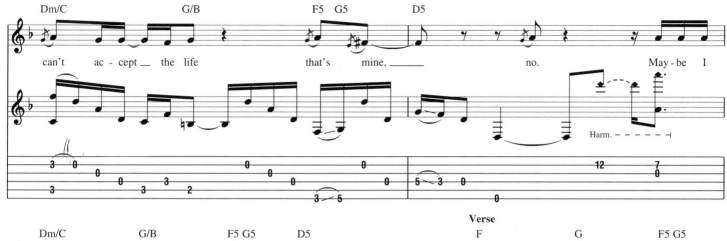

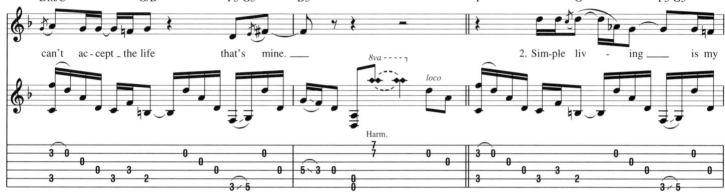

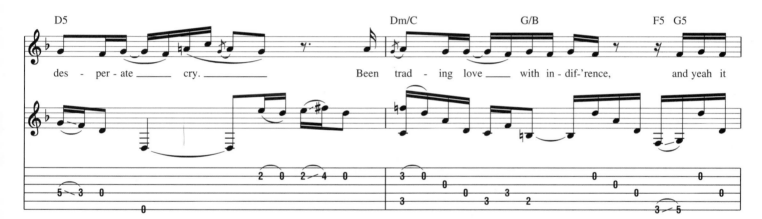

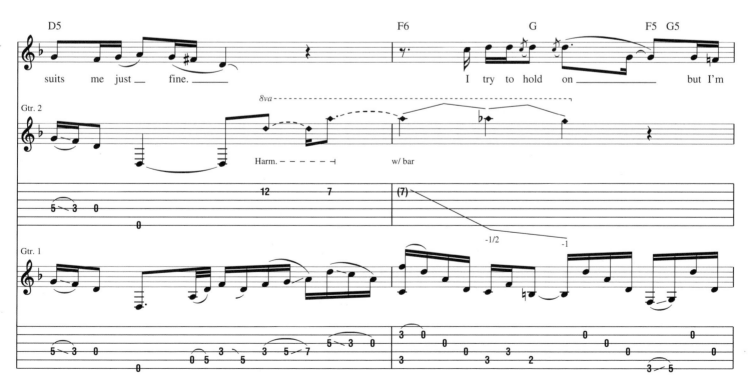

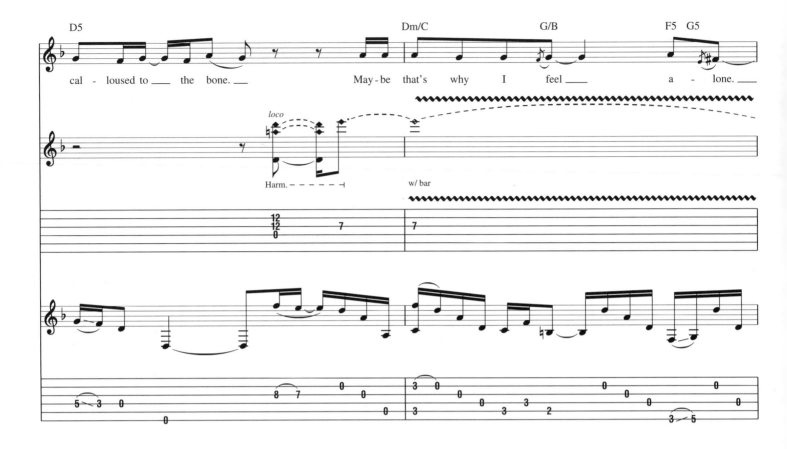

cal - loused to ____ the bone. ____ May - be that's why I feel ____ a - lone.

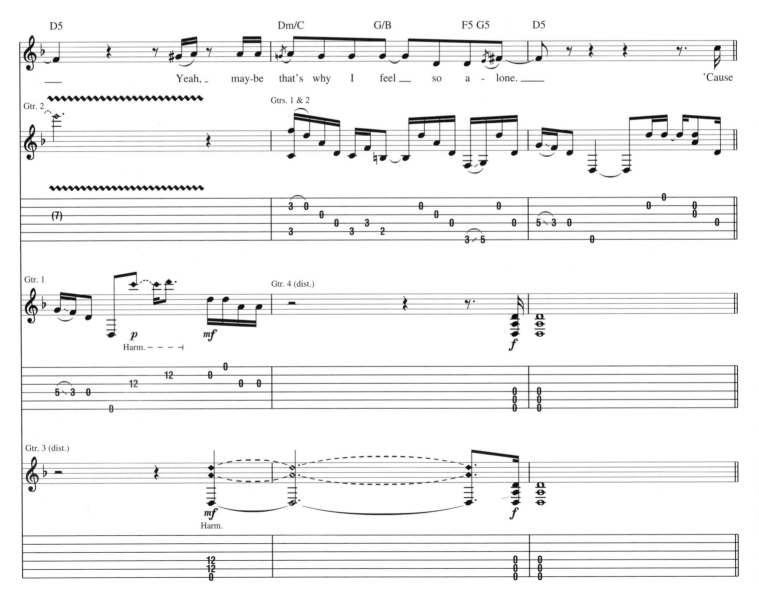

Yeah, ____ may-be that's why I feel ____ so a - lone. ____ 'Cause

Chorus

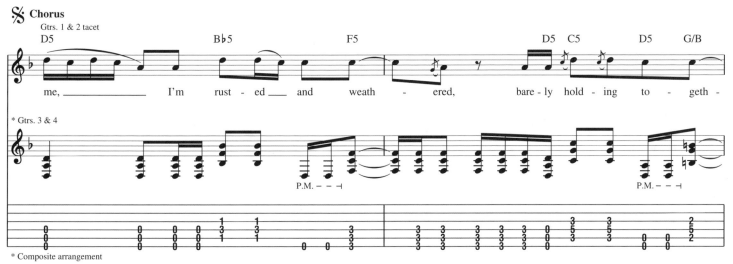

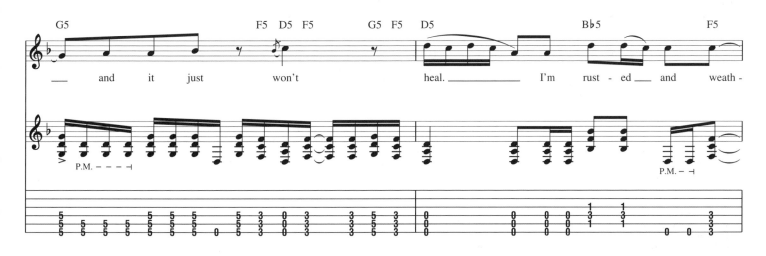

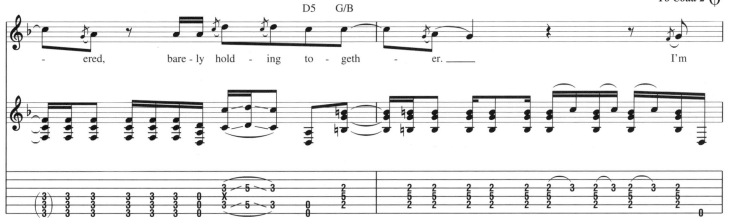

Verse

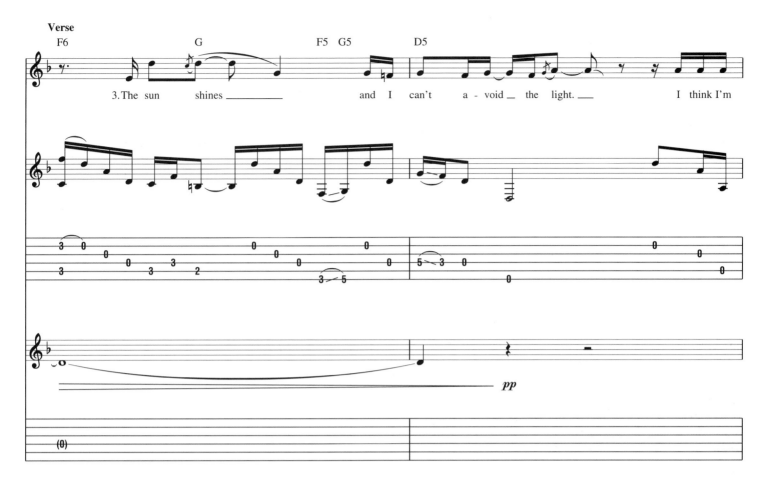

3. The sun shines _____ and I can't a-void _ the light. _ I think I'm

hold - ing on _ to life _ too tight. _

Ash - es to ash - es _ and dust to _____ dust. _

Some-times I feel __ like __ giv - ing up. _____ Yeah I said __

D.S. al Coda 1

some-times I feel ___ like _____ giv - ing up. ___ 'Cause

* Harmonic located eight-tenths the distance
between the 3rd & 4th frets.

Coda 1
Interlude

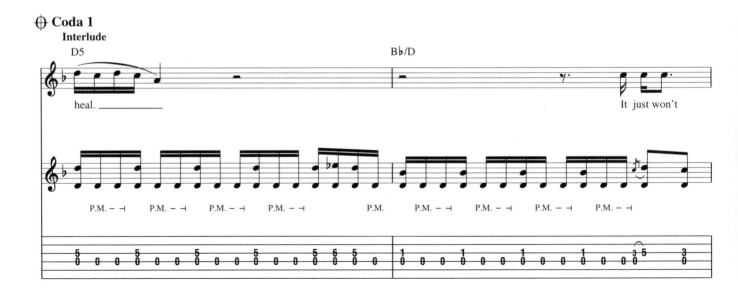

heal. _____ It just won't

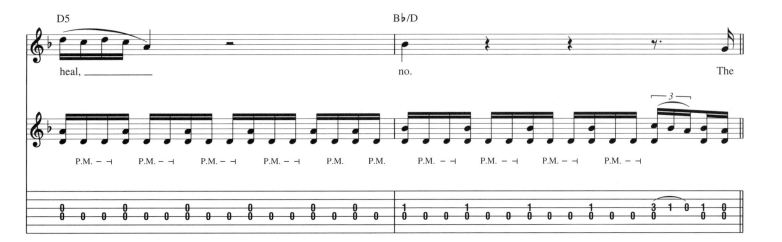

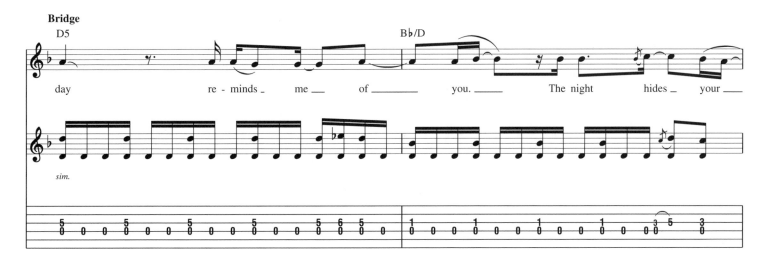

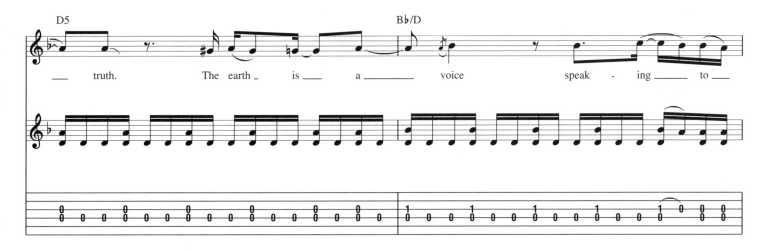

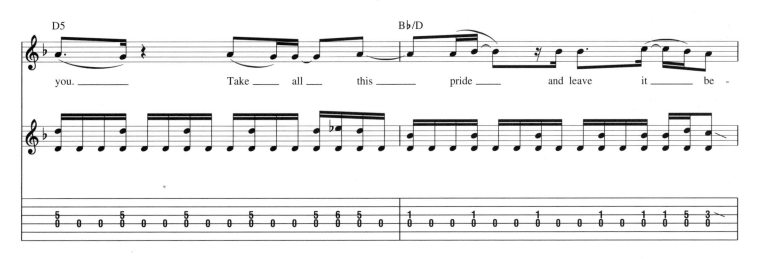

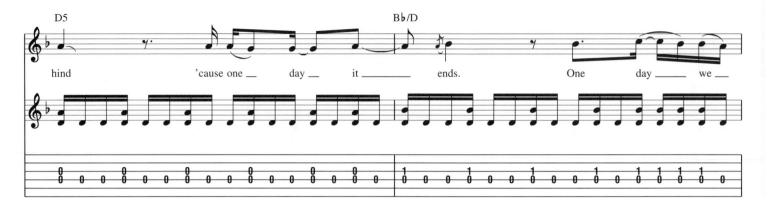

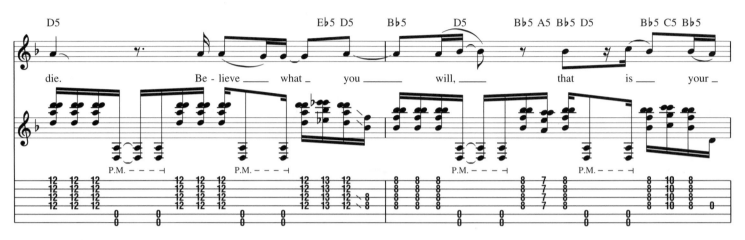

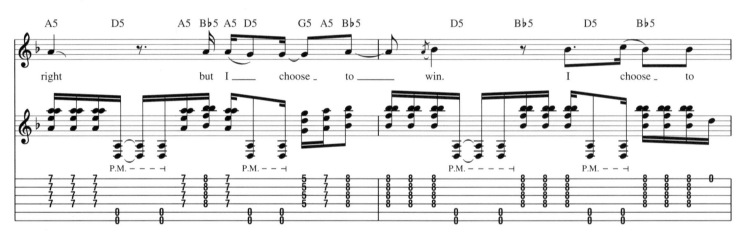

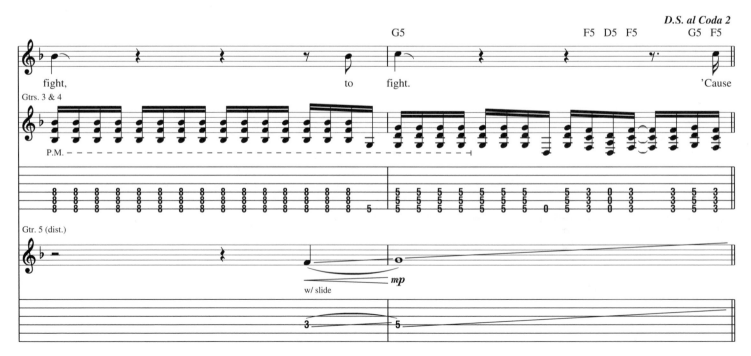

Coda 2
Outro

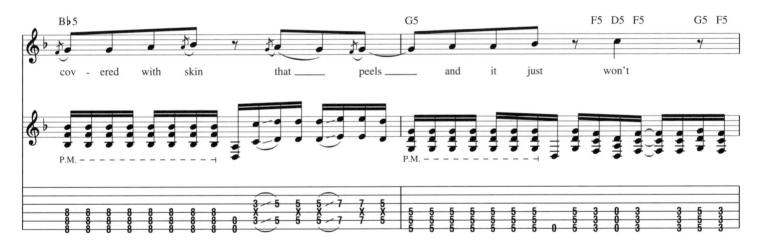

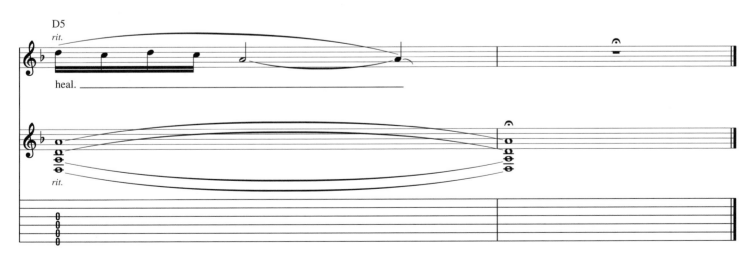

Hide

Words and Music by Mark Tremonti and Scott Stapp

Open B♭ tuning:
(low to high) F–B♭–F–B♭–D–F

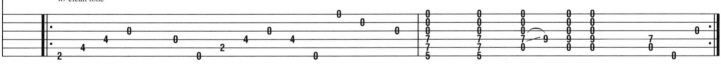

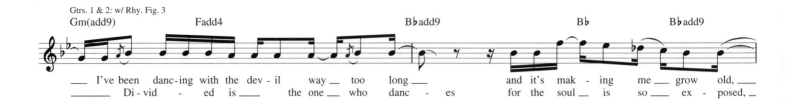

Gtrs. 1 & 2: w/ Rhy. Fig. 3

Gm(add9) Fadd4 B♭add9 B♭ B♭add9

___ I've been danc-ing with the dev-il way __ too long __ and it's mak-ing me grow old, __
___ Di-vid - ed is the one __ who danc - es for the soul __ is so ex - posed, __

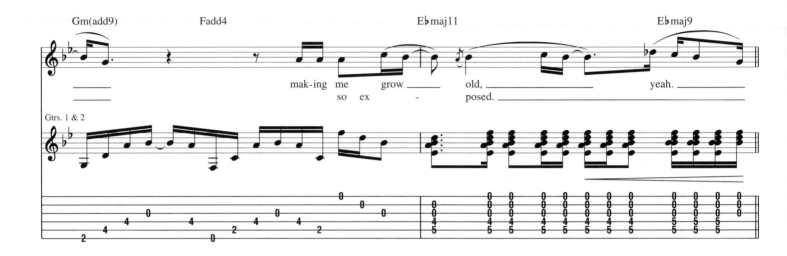

Gm(add9) Fadd4 E♭maj11 E♭maj9

mak-ing me grow __ old, __ yeah. ___
so ex - posed. ___

Gtrs. 1 & 2

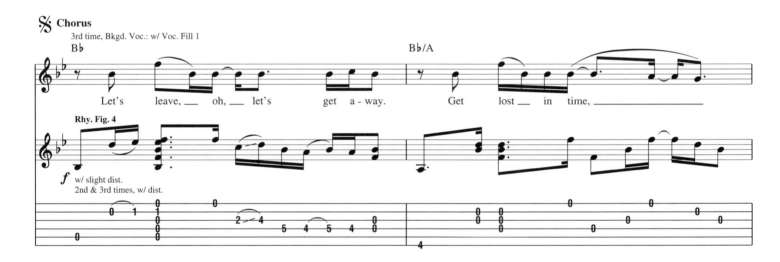

𝄋 Chorus

3rd time, Bkgd. Voc.: w/ Voc. Fill 1

B♭ B♭/A

Let's leave, __ oh, __ let's get a - way. Get lost __ in time, ___

Rhy. Fig. 4

f w/ slight dist.
2nd & 3rd times, w/ dist.

Gm(add9) Fadd4 E♭maj9 B♭/D E♭maj9

where__ there's no ___ rea - son left to ___ hide, ___ yeah.

End Rhy. Fig. 4

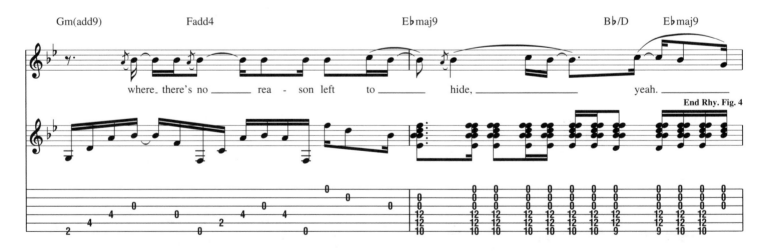

Voc. Fill 1

___

Don't Stop Dancing

Words and Music by Mark Tremonti and Scott Stapp

Pre-Chorus

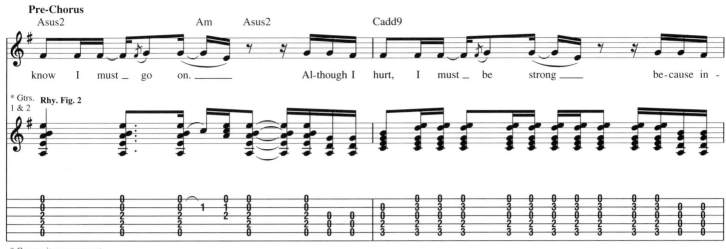

know I must _ go on. ____ Al-though I hurt, I must _ be strong ____ be-cause in -

* Composite arrangement

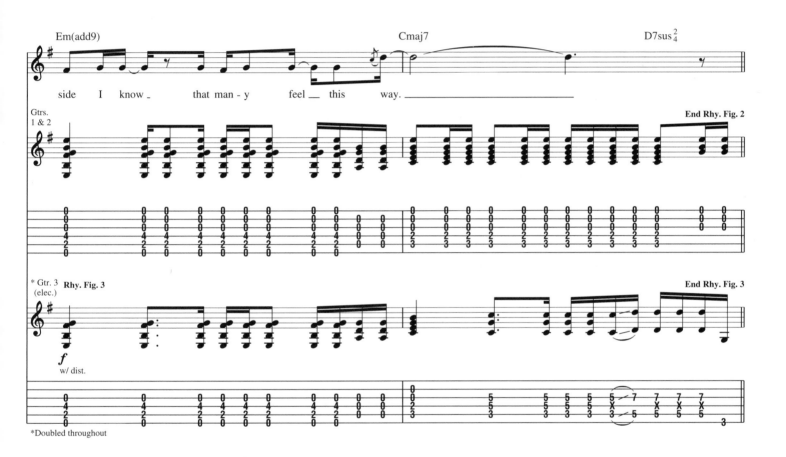

side I know _ that man - y feel _ this way. ____

*Doubled throughout

Chorus

Chil - dren, ____ don't ____ stop danc - ing. ____ Be - lieve _

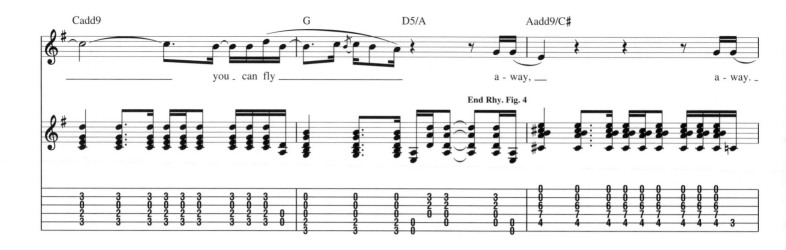

you _ can fly _____ a - way, _____ a - way. _

Interlude

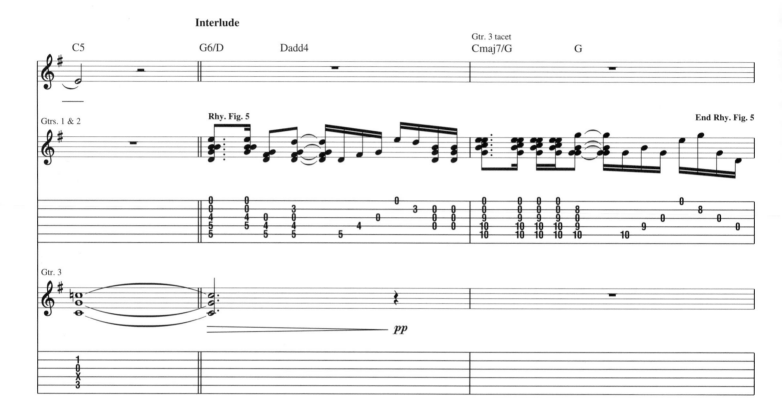

pp

Verse

2. At times life's un - fair ___ and you know _ it's plain _ to see. _

Hey God, I know _ I'm just a dot in this world. _ Have you for - got a - bout ___ me? _

What - ev - er life _ brings, I've been through ev - 'ry - thing and now I'm on my knees _ a - gain. But I

Pre-Chorus

know I must _ go on. ___ Al-though I hurt, I must _ be strong ___ be-cause in-

Chorus

side I know _ that man - y feel _ this way. ___ Chil - dren, ___ don't _ stop

danc - ing. ___ Be - lieve _____ you _ can fly _____ a - way, _

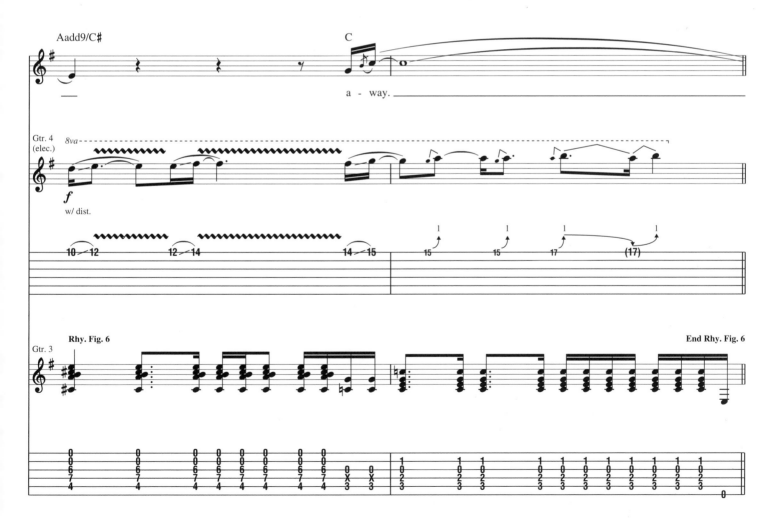

_ a - way. ___

Guitar Solo

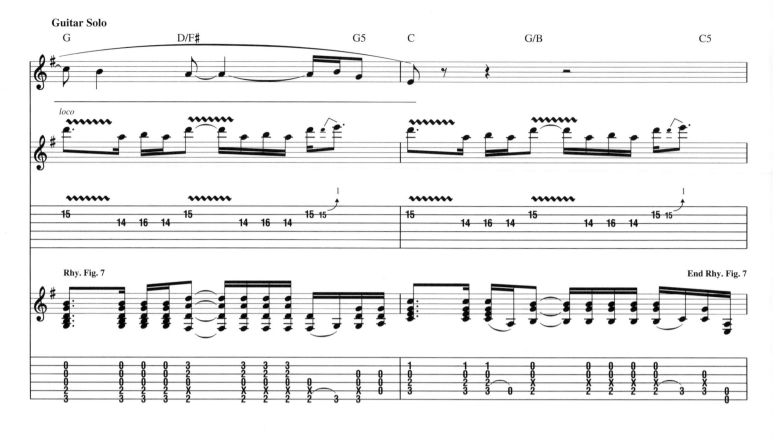

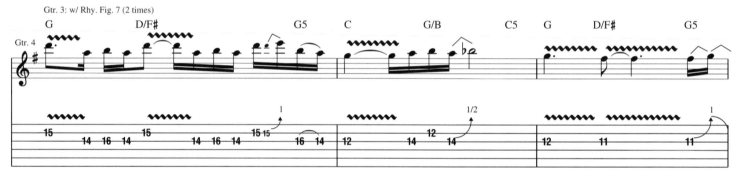

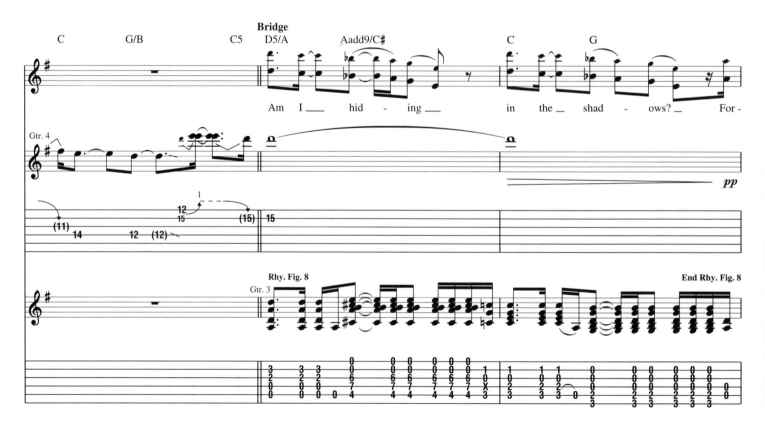

Am I ___ hid - ing ___ in the ___ shad - ows? ___ For -

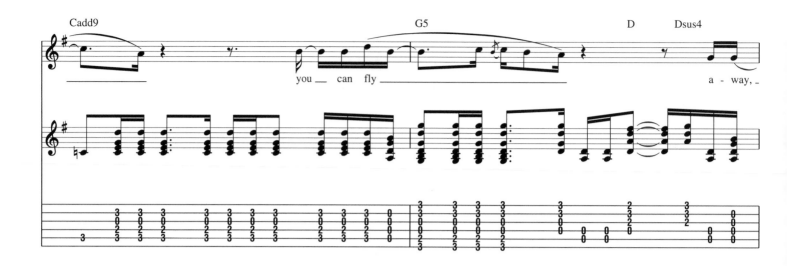

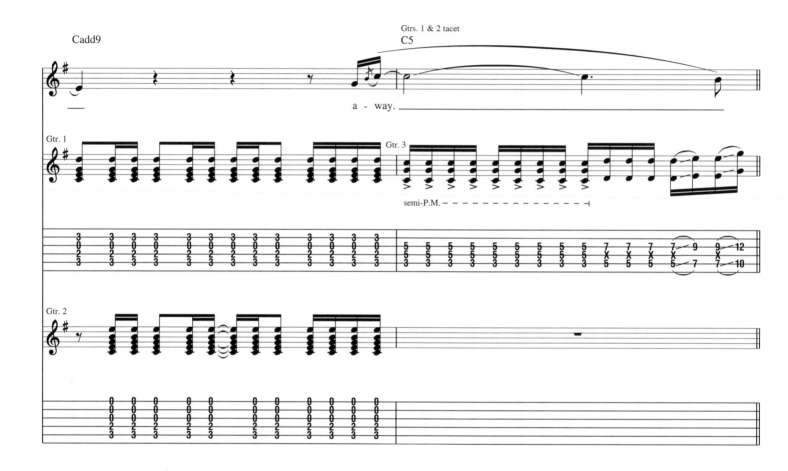

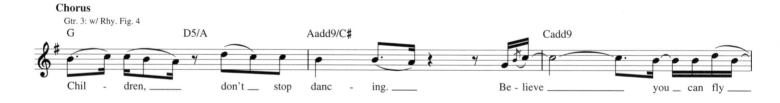

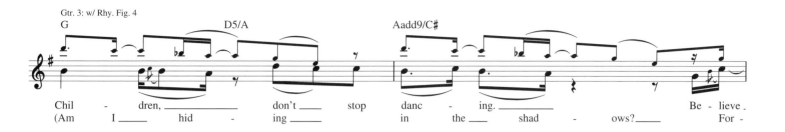

Gtr. 3: w/ Rhy. Fig. 4

Chil - dren, don't _____ stop danc - ing.
(Am I _____ hid - ing _____ in the _____ shad - ows?)

Be - lieve
For -

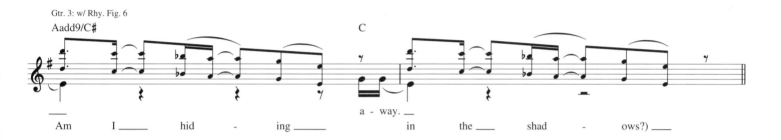

get the _____ pain _____ and
you can fly _____ for - get the _____ sor - rows. _____

a - way, _

Gtr. 3: w/ Rhy. Fig. 6

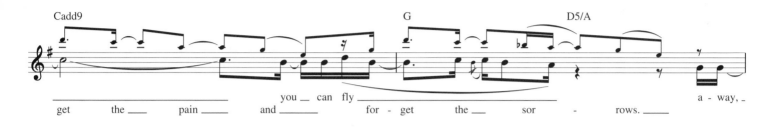

Am I _____ hid - ing _____ in the _____ shad - ows?) _____

a - way. _

Outro

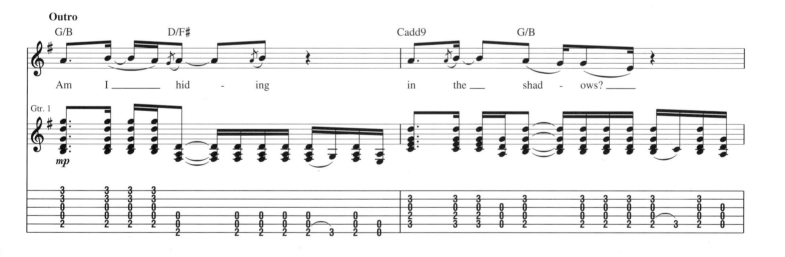

Am I _____ hid - ing in the _____ shad - ows? _____

Gtr. 1

mp

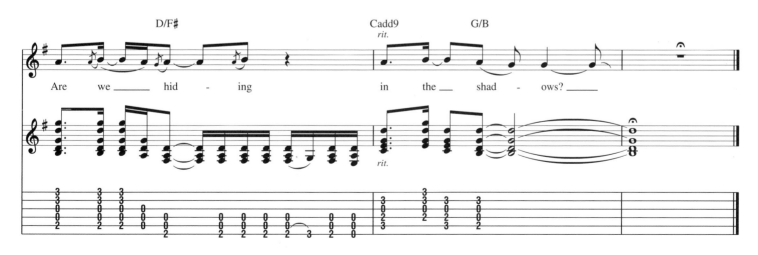

Are we _____ hid - ing in the _____ shad - ows? _____

rit.

Lullaby

Words and Music by Mark Tremonti and Scott Stapp

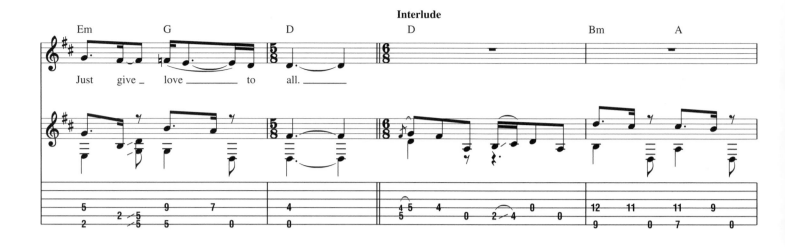

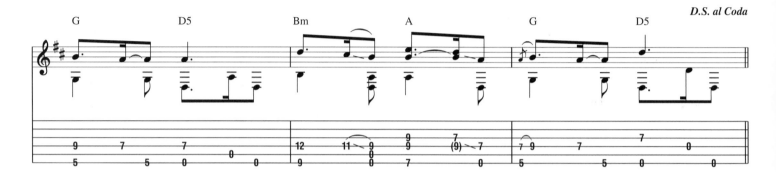

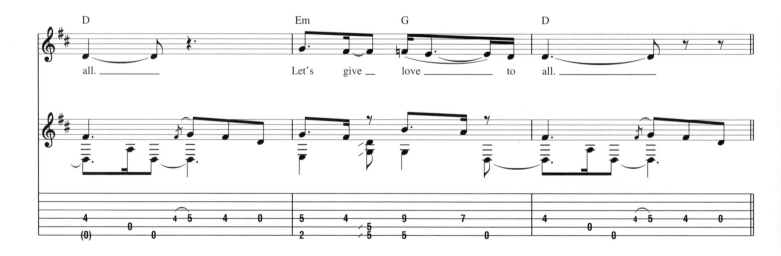

Guitar Notation Legend

Guitar Music can be notated three different ways: on a *musical staff*, in *tablature*, and in *rhythm slashes*.

RHYTHM SLASHES are written above the staff. Strum chords in the rhythm indicated. Use the chord diagrams found at the top of the first page of the transcription for the appropriate chord voicings. Round noteheads indicate single notes.

THE MUSICAL STAFF shows pitches and rhythms and is divided by bar lines into measures. Pitches are named after the first seven letters of the alphabet.

TABLATURE graphically represents the guitar fingerboard. Each horizontal line represents a string, and each number represents a fret.

4th string, 2nd fret   1st & 2nd strings open, played together   open D chord

HALF-STEP BEND: Strike the note and bend up 1/2 step.

WHOLE-STEP BEND: Strike the note and bend up one step.

GRACE NOTE BEND: Strike the note and immediately bend up as indicated.

SLIGHT (MICROTONE) BEND: Strike the note and bend up 1/4 step.

BEND AND RELEASE: Strike the note and bend up as indicated, then release back to the original note. Only the first note is struck.

PRE-BEND: Bend the note as indicated, then strike it.

VIBRATO: The string is vibrated by rapidly bending and releasing the note with the fretting hand.

WIDE VIBRATO: The pitch is varied to a greater degree by vibrating with the fretting hand.

HAMMER-ON: Strike the first (lower) note with one finger, then sound the higher note (on the same string) with another finger by fretting it without picking.

PULL-OFF: Place both fingers on the notes to be sounded. Strike the first note and without picking, pull the finger off to sound the second (lower) note.

LEGATO SLIDE: Strike the first note and then slide the same fret-hand finger up or down to the second note. The second note is not struck.

SHIFT SLIDE: Same as legato slide, except the second note is struck.

TRILL: Very rapidly alternate between the notes indicated by continuously hammering on and pulling off.

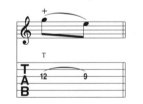

TAPPING: Hammer ("tap") the fret indicated with the pick-hand index or middle finger and pull off to the note fretted by the fret hand.

NATURAL HARMONIC: Strike the note while the fret-hand lightly touches the string directly over the fret indicated.

PINCH HARMONIC: The note is fretted normally and a harmonic is produced by adding the edge of the thumb or the tip of the index finger of the pick hand to the normal pick attack.

PICK SCRAPE: The edge of the pick is rubbed down (or up) the string, producing a scratchy sound.

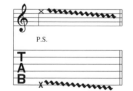

MUFFLED STRINGS: A percussive sound is produced by laying the fret hand across the string(s) without depressing, and striking them with the pick hand.

PALM MUTING: The note is partially muted by the pick hand lightly touching the string(s) just before the bridge.

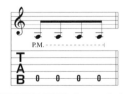

RAKE: Drag the pick across the strings indicated with a single motion.

TREMOLO PICKING: The note is picked as rapidly and continuously as possible.

VIBRATO BAR DIVE AND RETURN: The pitch of the note or chord is dropped a specified number of steps (in rhythm) then returned to the original pitch.

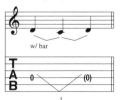

VIBRATO BAR SCOOP: Depress the bar just before striking the note, then quickly release the bar.

VIBRATO BAR DIP: Strike the note and then immediately drop a specified number of steps, then release back to the original pitch.

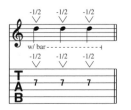

RECORDED VERSIONS
The Best Note-For-Note Transcriptions Available

ALL BOOKS INCLUDE TABLATURE

00690501 Adams, Bryan – Greatest Hits $19.95
00692015 Aerosmith – Greatest Hits $22.95
00690488 Aerosmith – Just Push Play $19.95
00690178 Alice in Chains – Acoustic $19.95
00694865 Alice in Chains – Dirt $19.95
00694925 Alice in Chains – Jar of Flies/Sap $19.95
00690387 Alice in Chains – Nothing Safe –
　　　　　　The Best of the Box $19.95
00694932 Allman Brothers Band – Volume 1 .....$24.95
00694933 Allman Brothers Band – Volume 2 .....$24.95
00694934 Allman Brothers Band – Volume 3 .....$24.95
00690513 American Hi-Fi $19.95
00694878 Atkins, Chet – Vintage Fingerstyle $19.95
00690418 Audio Adrenaline, Best of $17.95
00690366 Bad Company Original Anthology - Bk 1 .$19.95
00690367 Bad Company Original Anthology - Bk 2 .$19.95
00694929 Beatles: 1962-1966 ....$24.95
00694930 Beatles: 1967-1970 ....$24.95
00694880 Beatles – Abbey Road $19.95
00690110 Beatles – Book 1 (White Album) $19.95
00694832 Beatles – For Acoustic Guitar $19.95
00660140 Beatles – Guitar Book $19.95
00694863 Beatles –
　　　　　　Sgt. Pepper's Lonely Hearts Club Band ..$19.95
00690397 Beck – Midnite Vultures $19.95
00694884 Benson, George – Best of $19.95
00692385 Berry, Chuck $19.95
00692200 Black Sabbath –
　　　　　　We Sold Our Soul for Rock 'N' Roll ...$19.95
00690305 Blink 182 – Dude Ranch $19.95
00690389 Blink 182 – Enema of the State $19.95
00690523 Blink 182 – Take Off Your Pants & Jacket .$19.95
00690028 Blue Oyster Cult – Cult Classics $19.95
00690168 Buchanan, Roy – Collection $19.95
00690491 Bowie, David – Best of $19.95
00690451 Buckley, Jeff – Collection $24.95
00690364 Cake – Songbook $19.95
00690293 Chapman, Steven Curtis – Best of $19.95
00690043 Cheap Trick – Best of $19.95
00690171 Chicago – Definitive Guitar Collection ...$22.95
00690415 Clapton Chronicles – Best of Eric Clapton .$18.95
00690393 Clapton, Eric – Selections from Blues $19.95
00690074 Clapton, Eric – The Cream of Clapton ..$24.95
00690010 Clapton, Eric – From the Cradle $19.95
00660139 Clapton, Eric – Journeyman $19.95
00694869 Clapton, Eric – Unplugged $22.95
00694896 Clapton, Eric/John Mayall – Bluesbreakers .$19.95
00690162 Clash, Best of $19.95
00690494 Coldplay – Parachutes $19.95
00694940 Counting Crows – August & Everything After $19.95
00694840 Cream – Disraeli Gears $19.95
00690401 Creed – Human Clay $19.95
00690352 Creed – My Own Prison $19.95
00690484 dc Talk – Intermission: The Greatest Hits .$19.95
00690289 Deep Purple, Best of $17.95
00690384 Di Franco, Ani – Best of $19.95
00690322 Di Franco, Ani – Little Plastic Castle ...$19.95
00690380 Di Franco, Ani – Up Up Up Up Up Up $19.95
00695382 Dire Straits – Sultans of Swing $19.95
00690347 Doors, The – Anthology $22.95
00690348 Doors, The – Essential Guitar Collection .$16.95
00690349 Etheridge, Melissa – Skin $19.95
00690349 Eve 6 ....$19.95
00690496 Everclear, Best of $19.95
00690515 Extreme II – Pornograffitti $19.95
00690323 Fastball – All the Pain Money Can Buy ...$19.95
00690235 Foo Fighters – The Colour and the Shape .$19.95

00690394 Foo Fighters –
　　　　　　There Is Nothing Left to Lose $19.95
00690222 G3 Live – Satriani, Vai, Johnson $22.95
00690536 Garbage – Beautiful Garbage $19.95
00690438 Genesis Guitar Anthology $19.95
00690338 Goo Goo Dolls – Dizzy Up the Girl $19.95
00690114 Guy, Buddy – Collection Vol. A-J $22.95
00690193 Guy, Buddy – Collection Vol. L-Y $22.95
00694798 Harrison, George – Anthology $19.95
00692930 Hendrix, Jimi – Are You Experienced? ..$24.95
00692931 Hendrix, Jimi – Axis: Bold As Love $22.95
00694944 Hendrix, Jimi – Blues $24.95
00692932 Hendrix, Jimi – Electric Ladyland $24.95
00690218 Hendrix, Jimi – First Rays of the New Rising Sun $27.95
00690017 Hendrix, Jimi – Woodstock $24.95
00660029 Holly, Buddy $19.95
00690054 Hootie & The Blowfish –
　　　　　　Cracked Rear View $19.95
00690457 Incubus – Make Yourself $19.95
00690544 Incubus – Morningview $19.95
00690136 Indigo Girls – 1200 Curfews $22.95
00694833 Joel, Billy – For Guitar $19.95
00694912 Johnson, Eric – Ah Via Musicom $19.95
00694799 Johnson, Robert – At the Crossroads ...$19.95
00690271 Johnson, Robert – The New Transcriptions $24.95
00699131 Joplin, Janis – Best of $19.95
00693185 Judas Priest – Vintage Hits $19.95
00690444 King, B.B. and Eric Clapton –
　　　　　　Riding with the King $19.95
00690339 Kinks, The – Best of $19.95
00690279 Liebert, Ottmar + Luna Negra –
　　　　　　Opium Highlights $19.95
00694755 Malmsteen, Yngwie – Rising Force $19.95
00694956 Marley, Bob – Legend $19.95
00694945 Marley, Bob – Songs of Freedom $24.95
00690283 McLachlan, Sarah – Best of $19.95
00690382 McLachlan, Sarah – Mirrorball $19.95
00690239 Matchbox 20 – Mad Season $19.95
00690239 Matchbox 20 – Yourself or Someone Like You .$19.95
00694952 Megadeth – Countdown to Extinction ...$19.95
00690391 Megadeth – Risk $19.95
00694951 Megadeth – Rust in Peace $22.95
00690495 Megadeth – The World Needs a Hero ...$19.95
00690040 Miller, Steve, Band – Greatest Hits $19.95
00690448 MxPx – The Ever Passing Moment $19.95
00690189 Nirvana – From the Muddy
　　　　　　Banks of the Wishkah $19.95
00694913 Nirvana – In Utero $19.95
00694883 Nirvana – Nevermind $19.95
00690026 Nirvana – Unplugged™ in New York ...$19.95
00690121 Oasis – (What's the Story) Morning Glory .$19.95
00690358 Offspring, The – Americana $19.95
00690485 Offspring, The – Conspiracy of One $19.95
00690203 Offspring, The – Smash $18.95
00694847 Osbourne, Ozzy – Best of $22.95
00694830 Osbourne, Ozzy – No More Tears $19.95
00690538 Oysterhead – The Grand Pecking Order ..$19.95
00694855 Pearl Jam – Ten $19.95
00690439 Perfect Circle, A – Mer De Noms $19.95
00690176 Phish – Billy Breathes $22.95
00690424 Phish – Farmhouse $19.95
00690240 Phish – Hoist $19.95
00690331 Phish – Story of the Ghost $19.95
00690428 Pink Floyd – Dark Side of the Moon $19.95
00690456 P.O.D. – The Fundamental
　　　　　　Elements of Southtown $19.95
00693864 Police, The – Best of $19.95

00690299 Presley, Elvis – Best of Elvis:
　　　　　　The King of Rock 'n' Roll $19.95
00694975 Queen – Greatest Hits $24.95
00694910 Rage Against the Machine $19.95
00690395 Rage Against the Machine –
　　　　　　The Battle of Los Angeles $19.95
00690145 Rage Against the Machine – Evil Empire ..$19.95
00690478 Rage Against the Machine – Renegades ...$19.95
00690426 Ratt – Best of $19.95
00690055 Red Hot Chili Peppers –
　　　　　　Bloodsugarsexmagik $19.95
00690379 Red Hot Chili Peppers – Californication ..$19.95
00690090 Red Hot Chili Peppers – One Hot Minute ..$22.95
00694899 R.E.M. – Automatic for the People $19.95
00690014 Rolling Stones – Exile on Main Street ...$24.95
00690135 Rush, Otis – Collection $19.95
00690502 Saliva – Every Six Seconds $19.95
00690031 Santana's Greatest Hits $19.95
00120123 Shepherd, Kenny Wayne – Trouble Is ...$19.95
00690419 Slipknot $19.95
00690530 Slipknot – Iowa $19.95
00690330 Social Distortion – Live at the Roxy $19.95
00690385 Sonicflood $19.95
00694957 Stewart, Rod – Unplugged...And Seated ..$22.95
00690021 Sting – Fields of Gold $19.95
00690519 Sum 41 – All Killer No Filler $19.95
00690425 System of a Down $19.95
00690531 System of a Down – Toxicity $19.95
00694824 Taylor, James – Best of $16.95
00690238 Third Eye Blind $19.95
00690403 Third Eye Blind – Blue $19.95
00690295 Tool – Aenima $19.95
00690039 Vai, Steve – Alien Love Secrets $24.95
00690343 Vai, Steve – Flex-able Leftovers $19.95
00660137 Vai, Steve – Passion & Warfare $24.95
00690392 Vai, Steve – The Ultra Zone $19.95
00690370 Vaughan, Stevie Ray and Double Trouble –
　　　　　　The Real Deal: Greatest Hits Volume 2 ...$22.95
00690455 Vaughan, Stevie Ray – Blues at Sunrise ..$19.95
00690116 Vaughan, Stevie Ray – Guitar Collection ..$24.95
00660136 Vaughan, Stevie Ray – In Step $19.95
00660058 Vaughan, Stevie Ray –
　　　　　　Lightnin' Blues 1983-1987 ....$24.95
00690417 Vaughan, Stevie Ray – Live at Carnegie Hall $19.95
00694835 Vaughan, Stevie Ray – The Sky Is Crying ..$22.95
00690015 Vaughan, Stevie Ray – Texas Flood $19.95
00120026 Walsh, Joe – Look What I Did... ......$24.95
00694789 Waters, Muddy – Deep Blues $24.95
00690071 Weezer $19.95
00690516 Weezer (The Green Album) $19.95
00690286 Weezer – Pinkerton $19.95
00690447 Who, The – Best of $24.95
00690320 Williams, Dar – Best of $17.95
00690319 Wonder, Stevie – Some of the Best $17.95
00690443 Zappa, Frank – Hot Rats $19.95